TALKING ABOUT
MYSELF

MY FAMILY

Interviews by Angela Neustatter
Photographs by Laurence Cendrowicz

W
FRANKLIN WATTS
LONDON•SYDNEY

First published in 2008 by Franklin Watts

Franklin Watts,
338 Euston Road,
London, NW1 3BH

Franklin Watts Australia,
Level 17/207 Kent Street,
Sydney, NSW 2000

Series editor: Sarah Peutrill
Art Director: Jonathan Hair
Design: Elaine Wilkinson
Panels written by: Sarah Ridley
Researcher: Charlotte Wormald
Photographs: Laurence Cendrowicz (unless otherwise stated)

The Author and Publisher would like to thank the interviewees for
their contributions to this book. Also thanks to Anita Bennett.

Picture credits: absolut/Shutterstock: 16. Olly Hoeben: 14. Rob
Marmion/Shutterstock: 21. ronfromyork/Shutterstock: 24.
Shutterstock: 15. Andrew Skinner/Shutterstock: 19. Clive
Watkins/Shutterstock: 12. Every attempt has been made to clear
copyright. Should there be any inadvertent omission please apply
to the publisher for rectification.

Dewey number: 306.85

ISBN: 978 0 7496 7706 0

Printed in China

Franklin Watts is a division of Hachette Children's Books,
an Hachette Livre UK company.

CONTENTS

WHAT IS A FAMILY?

Thirty years ago a family almost always meant parents and children living in a home together. But although many people still choose this traditional arrangement, today families are many different things including lone parent families, stepfamilies, and even gay parents.

Lone parent families

One in four children lives with a single parent for a variety of reasons, such as separation, divorce or death. There can be a lot of negative stuff in the news about how children in one-parent families do less well than children with two parents. However, a great many lone parent families are strong and happy and research shows that children in lone parent families are often more independent and mature than their peers. It is a fact that nearly half of all one-parent families in the UK are below the government-defined poverty line. This can affect how much time, energy and emotional resources the parent has available for children. In exceptional cases a child may have to grow up too fast – as our young carer Sauska (page 26) had to.

Divorce and stepfamilies

With 40% of marriages ending in divorce, a great many children have to deal with parental conflict, their own pain, disruption and split loyalties. Children quite often feel shame and embarrassment and do not want to talk about what is going on. Children may show bad behaviour and emotional difficulties. As Tegan describes (page 14), children may feel they have to try to make everything all right for

parents who are clearly unhappy themselves, and this can be a great responsibility for a young person. Even young adults can find parents divorcing traumatic, as Melanie found out (page 16).

When couples divorce, quite often one or both will find a new partner and create a stepfamily. More than one-in-ten of all families with dependent children in Britain are stepfamilies. This means the children have to adjust to a new family life, possibly moving house or school and living with different rules and routines and often step-siblings. While the idea of other children in the family may sound fun, the reality can be rather harder. Quite often children who are already upset at their parents splitting up feel angry and resentful at what has happened and don't want to be friends with step-siblings. Children may feel it unfair that their own parent should give time and attention to other children. This is a perfectly normal reaction.

The good news is that a significant number of children and young adults report that, once their family life has settled down again, things are better than when their mother and father were together and miserable.

Adoption and fostering

More than a quarter of a million children are classed as at risk at any one time in Britain. The majority of these are because there are worrying signs including neglect or physical and emotional abuse in their home. Some of these children are taken into local authority care. They may live in a care home or they may be found a foster home until they can go back to their own homes. Some may leave their family altogether and be adopted by a new family. Evidence shows that if foster and adoptive parents are understanding they can help these children cope with the trauma they may have experienced being removed from their biological families, and become secure and happy.

Happy families?

However different to the traditional model, most families are usually good places for children to grow up healthy and happy. A BBC poll on changing families found that whatever the re-shaping and challenges families face these days, 93% judged their family life to be fairly or very happy.

However, if you are not happy at home; if you suffer depression or anger and violent feelings; if you feel alienated from parents or if a member of the family is being abusive to you; if you are witnessing or experiencing domestic violence; if you feel suicidal, or if you simply feel you need support through a difficult time, it is important that you seek help. There is a list of places you can contact on page 31.

DEALING WITH DIVORCE

Alex, 14, was four when his parents divorced. He lives with his mother and sees his father once a week. He has had to adjust to the contrast between the way his two parents live.

I live with my mum and my brother and she takes care of me so she is the one who has to be strict, have guidelines and all that. Mum gets me to school, makes sure I have the right clothes, sorts out problems, sees I get my homework done, makes my supper, things like that.

But when I go to my dad at weekends it's quite different – more relaxed. I see that he can be the good guy and have fun with me and not worry about the things that Mum has to. For example if there's a problem with my schoolwork or if I have done something stupid my dad's line is 'oh boys will be boys' but my mum will be much more upset and then they bicker a bit. But it's never rude or malicious. They've never said nasty things about each other in front of us.

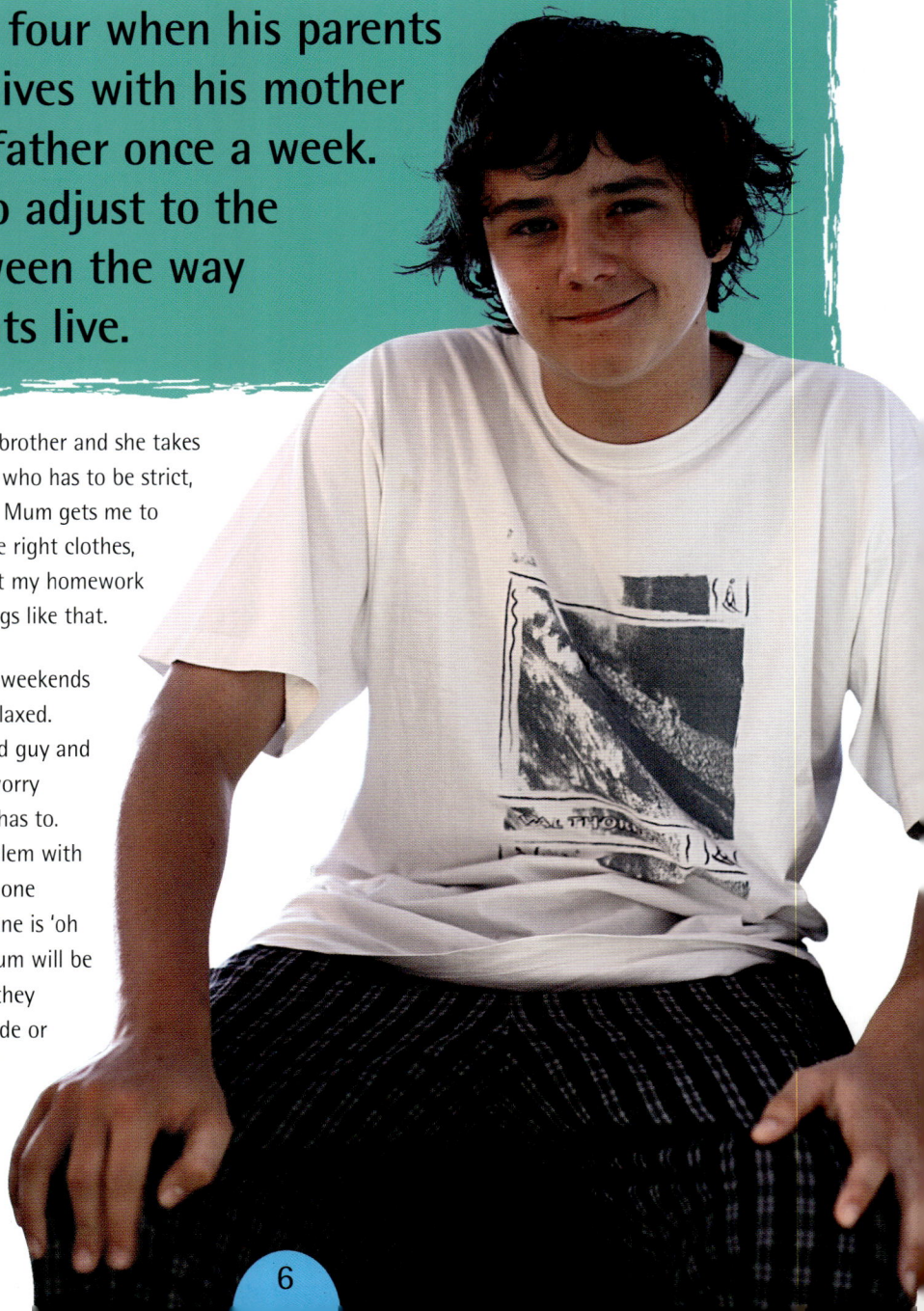

With Dad we quite often eat out and perhaps we'll come back and watch a DVD – he's got a huge collection – and we relax and chat while watching. Or else we might go out for one of the weekend days to visit some of his family, or to some special place.

Different lifestyles

My parents have very different living styles. My dad is pretty well off. He has a huge apartment and he has loads of gadgets. He works in a high-powered job with computers. And he is very smooth, very James Bond-ish. He drinks martini and blends into most parties and social scenes.

My mum works for the NHS as a PA and she seems less happy than Dad. She's no way as well off and doesn't have much in the way of gadgets. Not even a TV, but I do have a computer at home. It can feel a bit of a contrast going between the two, but I feel at home in my mum's place and my friends live around there.

My parents have new partners. Mum split with someone after four years. I felt sad because I really got on with him and now there's someone new. I find that a bit weird. I can't see how you break up with someone after such a long time and immediately move on to someone else. My dad has been with his partner since I was tiny and I like her a lot.

Brother's support

When I'm feeling in conflict about our parents, or fed up with them, I talk to my brother although it tends not to be in great depth because we both accept what is done is done. My brother has shown me how to deal with things. For example if Mum and Dad have completely different views about something that needs deciding I'll often take my brother's judgement. The situation has made us close. ■

WHEN MY PARENTS SPLIT UP

When 10-year-old Isabel's* parents divorced she feared she would lose contact with her father. But she has been able to have a good relationship with both parents.

*Not her real name.

I was eight when my parents split up. I didn't understand what was happening except that my mum was very angry indeed and telling Dad to go. In fact they had split before but then they got back together again. They seemed happy and I was really happy then. But this time it was clear Mum meant it and Dad was very upset. My older sister and brother and I just hugged each other.

Dad moves out

My dad went to live in a flat and I lived with my mum in the family house. I spent most nights crying. I didn't

"I spent most nights crying. I didn't get much sleep and I was very miserable."

get much sleep and I was very miserable. Mum was in a bad state. I heard her crying at night and I tried to cut out the noise by putting a pillow over my head. I talked to my sister because we are very close and we comforted each other. Most nights when I was upset I slept in her bed or she was in mine.

Mum told my school-teacher what had happened and the teacher comforted me when I was sad in the playground. It would have been harder without this understanding at school.

Too scared to ask

I felt frightened I might lose touch with Dad altogether now he had gone for real. I didn't dare say this to him in case he said it was true. I talked to my best friend whose parents are still together and she was very helpful. She said, "Nothing will change in that way, you'll still see your dad."

And she was right. I go to see him very regularly and I can have friends to stay there, and it feels good.

Dad's new girlfriend

Dad has a new girlfriend he lives with and I like her. She's not an evil stepmother. She's nice to me. The first time I went to visit I didn't want to tell Mum I liked Dad's girlfriend because I feared she wouldn't like me any more, or she would get upset. But after a while when Mum was fine it seemed all right to do so and she was perfectly all right with it. She said, "Nothing will upset me now."

Things aren't difficult now except when Mum gets annoyed with Dad and criticises him. I don't like Dad being criticised. I told Mum this.

I don't dream of my parents being together any more. I have a good relationship with my dad but just in a different place. At Christmas my parents take it in turns to have us for the day. And even though Mum doesn't have anyone else, I don't feel I have to look after her. I feel she's handled everything well. And when my friends' parents are divorcing I am able to help them. ∎

DIVORCE

Thousands of married couples get divorced every year when their marriage has broken down to such a degree that it cannot be brought back together again. Divorce is the legal process that ends their marriage.

SPLITTING UP FOR GOOD

The process of getting divorced will involve making decisions about the children of the divorcing couple as well as splitting up possessions and money. If the couple cannot come to an agreement on these issues, mediators become involved. These trained professionals help a divorcing couple to reach an agreement about how much time the children will spend with each parent and how to split up their finances. If mediation does not work out, the court may have to make decisions for the couple. Usually it takes between four and eight months for a couple to get divorced but sorting out the financial side can take longer.

THE DECREES

The court makes a divorce final before the law. When the court is satisfied that the reasons for the divorce are proven, it will issue a decree nisi. A minimum of six weeks later, the court can issue a decree absolute which will legally end the marriage.

FATHER AND SON DIFFICULTIES

Francis, 16, has grown up with his sister and single mother. His father has never lived with them and he has had a very difficult relationship with his father.

Q How was family life?

My dad and mum weren't married and he had a daughter by a woman he met soon after I was born. There were two older children by a first marriage and he often had different girlfriends. I have just a few memories of going to Dad's cottage in Wales and Mum had another one nearby. He took me on walks and taught me to chop wood and I enjoyed that and there were other things. But he had a terrible temper that would suddenly explode and it was very frightening. And one time when he had given me food I was allergic to I was very sick in the night, and I had diarrhoea. I was crying and frightened but he wouldn't wake up and help me.

"... one time when he had given me food I was allergic to I was very sick in the night, and I had diarrhoea. I was crying and frightened but he wouldn't wake up and help me."

SEPARATED PARENTS

Many couples live together and have children together but do not marry. If their relationship breaks down, they separate – they do not get divorced as they were never married.

SEPARATION AGREEMENT
A separation agreement can be drawn up by the couple, usually with the help of a solicitor, sorting out the practical arrangements for the separation. It will cover financial arrangements for support of the children, agreements on where the children will live and how much they will see the parent that they don't live with, and will divide up possessions, including the house if they own one.

LEGAL SEPARATION
Some married couples choose to get separated, rather than legally divorced, if they no longer live together. If they wish to take this further, they can draw up a 'deed of separation' with solicitors, that sets out arrangements about the children, money, the house and possessions.

"Mum and Dad used to argue so I thought the less they saw of each other the better."

Q Did you ever wish he and your mother lived together?

No. Mum and Dad used to argue so I thought the less they saw of each other the better. Things got harder when Mum moved to Bristol. I was about seven then and I would visit Dad with my sister and Mum wasn't there to rescue us when he got angry. Mum explained that he'd had a very harsh upbringing and been sent to boarding school when he was six and that he had learned to shut down all his gentle feelings. I began to wish he'd just keep out of our lives. As I got older I

put up a fight when he came to collect me to go to Wales but Mum insisted I go because she thought it good for me to have a man's influence on my life.

Q Did you ever get close to your father?

When I was eight I spent a month on holiday with him. There were some good moments walking along the beach with him. I got close to Dad. But if I spoke to Mum on the phone and cried because I missed her he would get cross and tell me I was old enough not to do that. And when I got back home that changed. I felt upset he couldn't be like other dads I ▶

"He did come to rugby matches at my school a couple of times and I liked having him there watching, like a normal dad."

saw – interested in their children, taking them out to do fun things, wanting to talk to them. He did come to rugby matches at my school a couple of times and I liked having him there watching, like a normal dad.

Q Did he ever discuss your mother?

When I was younger he didn't talk about it but as I got older and started to argue with him he would say I was like Mum and criticise her, then I would stick up for

Mum and the arguments would get worse. Nothing he did actually made me think he cared about me in the way a dad should and I used to shout at Mum for having chosen him to be a father. He hardly ever paid any money to Mum for me, yet when Mum said I didn't have to see him, he went to court for visitation rights.

Q Was that a difficult time?

I became very unwell for half a year but nobody could say what was wrong. I was getting a lot of stomach aches, I couldn't sleep at night, I felt a lot of nausea. Dad didn't come once during this time. Mum took me to a psychiatrist and I talked about how scared I was when Dad dragged me out of the house to go to Wales and how I was frightened of Dad. I believed Mum hated me because she made me go. The psychiatrist told Mum I was old enough to decide not to see Dad if I wished and she agreed. I started to get better after that. And in the past three years I had the occasional email or card from Dad but nothing else, and that was great. I could concentrate on school and social life and feel good about life.

Q Do you imagine having a relationship with him in the future?

I have a bit of contact now and I think when I get to university I'll be more able to be an adult in how I deal with him. He will have something to offer because he is an intellectual and he values that in his children. ∎

BAD RELATIONS

Why do children begin to hate their parents? First of all children want their needs such as love, support, money and understanding to be fulfilled by their parents. If parents cannot do this, or curtail their freedom too much, the child may become dissatisfied, which may lead to dislike, and then to hate.

The second main reason comes from the circumstances the child is influenced by. This includes at home as well as outside. Sometimes parents have ongoing tiffs and arguments which disturb children. Friends are also an influence. Bad friends or people often affect their mind in a negative way and children lose respect for their parents.

IF YOU DON'T GET ON WITH A PARENT, HERE ARE SOME TIPS THAT MIGHT HELP:

- Talk to them – calmly, as often as you can.
- Don't assume they're out to get you.
- If they make rules you don't agree with, don't just flaunt them, negotiate, and be willing to compromise.
- Wait until you're calm to talk things through.
- Don't lie – if they catch you out they won't trust you again.
- Remind them of times when you were right or when you did act responsibly.
- Try talking to another adult, an older brother or sister, another member of the family, or family friend. See if you find it easier to tell them how you feel.
- Don't worry, relationships usually get better. If things are really bad, there's professional help available – see page 31.

KEEPING THE PEACE

Tegan was five and her sister Alexis was three when their parents separated. Tegan feels she took on the role of peacekeeper.

I don't remember much about the actual split. I've grown up knowing Mum in her townhouse and Dad in his country house. The difficult thing was they were on very bad terms. It used to upset me a lot when they were forever having arguments on the phone, and it made dividing our life between them quite difficult. I feel I have had to be the peacekeeper.

I think I have taken on the role of keeping my father and mother happy; it matters to me a lot that they should be. So I have tried very hard not to upset either of them and sometimes it has been so stressful trying to balance what felt right for me with what was right for my parents. It certainly hasn't made things easy growing up.

The trouble with Christmas

One thing that's always difficult is Christmas. I have always feared Mum would be offended if I spent it entirely with Dad. And I would feel so bad for Dad if we didn't spend time with him, so we do a lot of driving spending half the day with one, half with the other.

> "One thing that's always difficult is Christmas. I have always feared Mum would be offended if I spent it entirely with Dad."

Telling the truth

I have seen them both suffering although Mum hides it pretty well. Dad has wanted to talk about what happened more, and I think letting kids know what is going on is good, because it's frightening not to understand. But at times I felt it was all too adult for my sister and me. I feel I have had to protect her because she is very emotional and even now she comes to me with her problems. In the early days in bed at night she would ask me what was going to happen.

Seeing both sides

My mother has been very angry with Dad and because of that I didn't see his side of the story for a long time. It was difficult to hear Mum so hard on him. Now I'm older I have been able to see that he wasn't necessarily the bad guy. And they are both a bit calmer.

Regrets

The good thing is that they have always lived close by so we have the feeling of two homes, but we've always had less time with Dad and I regret that. I find it very sad to have no memory of being together as a family. I had a dream when I was younger of us all sitting under a tree and it was lovely.

We have had good parenting from Mum and Dad and I've never doubted they both love us. But Mum had a new boyfriend very soon after the split and we didn't like that. I remember my sister having a fit one time he was over. I think you need a period of adjustment before someone else is brought in.

It's been very painful at times but I think we have both turned out OK and what happened has made me determined to be very careful who I marry and to work hard at my own marriage. ■

DIFFICULT AT ANY AGE

Melanie* had just left home when her parents split up. Even though she was a young adult she found it very painful.

*Not her real name. Photo posed by model.

My parents always had a volatile relationship so I didn't realise things had got worse until it was blurted out that they were separating. It wasn't so much a huge shock as depressingly believable. Even so I was desperately upset and I told them to sort it out. Mum said I was getting ridiculously upset. I cried and cried and told Dad I couldn't believe it.

I remember when I was little they would have patches of great happiness but then a bad patch when Dad would close up, become very cold and not talk and Mum would be very emotional and angry. There were huge shouting matches.

First Christmas apart

The hardest thing was the breakdown of the family

"It wasn't so much a huge shock as depressingly believable."

Photo posed by model.

home and the first Christmas apart. I went back to university and I found it hard to talk to friends. I kept everything to myself and felt very upset and lonely. I didn't want to go home in the holidays so I went and stayed with my boyfriend.

In my final year Mum would call up and say to me that she could not handle what was going on. I got cross with her. I felt I needed her, particularly as I'd broken up with my boyfriend. But she hadn't any emotional space for me. And a while later she started seeing a married man and that made me very angry.

It's not my problem

I spoke to friends with divorced parents and they said it's hard but don't get involved. The most valuable thing said was, "It's not your problem". They saw I was thinking it was my problem and that everything I did affected how my parents behaved and felt. Then I started thinking if being separate would make them happy, perhaps I could be happy.

When I went down to see them from university it seemed Mum and Dad had achieved a sort of friendship with Dad staying in the house in his room a couple of nights a week. I hoped, and I think Mum did, that they'd get back together again. Then came the bombshell: Dad had a new partner. Everything fell apart. Mum wouldn't talk to Dad or see him after this.

Role reversal

Then Mum and I both got ill and that gave us something else to think about. Mum announced when she was better that we had to get over things. Dad was living in a cottage in the countryside with his girlfriend and was fine. But I wonder if they have understood that even if you are a young adult separation is an emotional trauma. You want to be sad and upset as if you were a child needing parents' comfort, but at the same time there's this role reversal where you feel you should be looking after them. You feel very alone and unprotected in the world. My parents both seem more settled and happy now, but I still haven't been able to feel the world is a safe place for my emotions. ∎

DIVORCE AND YOUNG ADULTS

When children are older teenagers or have already left home parents might assume that they will be less affected by the divorce. However, seeing your parents fight and break up is very upsetting, whatever your age. It can leave you feeling insecure. Your parents may ask you to take sides and they may be too consumed by their own emotions to notice the needs of you.

LIFE'S MORE COMPLICATED!
Having divorced parents can make simple decisions, such as where to spend Christmas, into emotional problems. It is hard to please both parents when they no longer live together and may have formed new relationships. Talking to friends or contacting one of the organisations listed on page 31, can help.

A 'NEW NORMAL'
Although many people struggle to cope with such a big change, in time a 'new normal' emerges. If your parents were very unhappy together you might even see a different side to them when they are no longer struggling to maintain a difficult marriage.

MEETING MY FATHER FOR THE FIRST TIME

Nell's mother was pregnant without knowing it when she and her boyfriend split up. Nell didn't meet her father until she was 24.

Q Did you decide to get in touch with your dad?

No. I'd heard about my dad wanting to get to know me through someone who used to work with him in a band. They mentioned me to my father who asked for my number.

Q How did that feel?

I was in shock. I had always thought about meeting him, mainly to be acknowledged, that I do exist. I had a good childhood, I was very close to my grandparents, and my mum – a single parent with no support financially or emotionally from my dad. She gave me so many opportunities as a child.

"I had always thought about meeting him, mainly to be acknowledged, that I do exist."

18

Q What happened next?

I found out he had a wife and two children that I didn't know about. I've never felt bitter about him and Mum splitting up, it was mutual and if it's not working it's best to move on. But I was disappointed that he chose to abandon his parental duties, whether you're with someone or not you have responsibilities. He chose to miss out.

Q Did you contact your father?

Yep, I didn't want to give my mobile number: so I set up an email address. He got back to me really quickly "Hi. I've been waiting a very long time to hear from you." I booked an appointment with my work counselling service. There we discussed the idea of a meeting and how I could prepare myself. I remember thinking, "Oh my God - this is really going to happen!"

Q So you met?

We met along the River Thames in London. I walked towards him, he said, "God look at you, you are beautiful, just like your grandma." He hugged me ▶

"There we discussed the idea of a meeting and how I could prepare myself. I remember thinking, 'Oh my God – this is really going to happen!'"

ESTRANGED PARENTS

Meeting up with a parent that you never knew as a child can be an exciting if nerve-wrecking experience. Finally you will see whether you are similar or different. You will be able to fill in 'holes' in your family history. You can seek answers to questions that have remained unanswered for many years. Many people hope that they will feel close to the estranged parent and that it will all be a positive experience.

EMOTIONAL ROLLERCOASTER
It can take people by surprise to see their father or mother for the first time. While it can be a tremendously happy time, it may also stir up bad feelings as you come to terms with the fact that the parent stopped seeing you, for whatever reason. Perhaps they have a new family and you discover you have half-brothers or sisters that you didn't even know about. Perhaps they have had a difficult life or a different life to the one you may have expected. The newly-found parent may want to tell you stories about their past, and the parent that brought you up, that might hurt you or them. It can be an unsettling time or a happy one, or both.

TRACING AN ESTRANGED PARENT
Should you wish to trace an estranged parent who has completely fallen out of contact, two national organisations may be able to help. The Salvation Army Family Tracing Service and Missing People both reunite hundreds of people every year and offer counselling and support, as well as a neutral place to meet. Their contact details are on page 31.

really tight. He was not what I expected. I imagined some tall man with long dreads. In photos he seemed darker-skinned, with long hair. He was tall, but he now had a shaved head. He took me to Marine Ices in Camden Town where he and my mum used to work. I remember feeling very unattached, probably the shock. He kept telling me I'd always been on his mind, so I asked the questions I wanted to know. I remember him talking a lot, but felt disappointed that he didn't ask me much about myself. At the end he asked when we would meet again. One of my fears is rejection, I assumed he hadn't tried to find me because he didn't want to. Then we made another date to meet.

Q Did things go well?

I was much more emotional before this meeting and I had had time to digest. I had a lot of anger and mixed feelings. He had done a lot of talking about himself the first time, and the next time he told me about the difficulties between himself and his present wife, so I realised it wasn't all the perfect family. There was a part of me that felt glad Mum wasn't with him, because he seemed like hard work. I also knew I needed to tell him more about myself. At the second meeting, I asked at what point he decided to cut me out of his life, because he had had some contact after I was born. He made some airy excuse about it being difficult with his wife and work problems – that struck me as a cop-out excuse. When he dropped me off he said he was never going to let me out of sight now. I remember thinking that he told me all the stuff people hope to hear, but I didn't feel a connection.

Q Was there another meeting?

For my birthday he booked a box at the Emirates stadium to see an Arsenal football match. It was straight after work, and I remember feeling irritable after a busy day. Since then I've become friends on Facebook with my brother and sister. It's weird seeing their pictures before I've even met them. There's a section where you have to say how you know someone, so it was nice when it came up with 'Nell is my sister'.

Q What about you and your dad now?

I've had no contact with my dad for six months now; he rang quite a bit at first but when I didn't phone back the calls stopped coming. I hope he's realised that it happened quite quickly and was getting to me a bit, that's why I stepped back. Right now I'm looking out for myself, I'm sure when we're both ready we'll meet again. ∎

CARE AND ADOPTION

James*, 21, was put into care aged four after very difficult early years and his feelings shut down. Sue and Jim adopted him aged eight and with them he has learned how to feel and care.

*Not his real name.

Q How many homes were you in before you were adopted?

James: I don't remember, I seemed to be moved a lot. I came to Sue and Jim, my adoptive Mum and Dad, with my brother Darren who was six.

Sue: James couldn't trust anyone. His birth family were very dysfunctional and neglected him badly. And his foster carers didn't seem to have any interest in his emotional needs. When he came to us he was shut away in his own little world. He hid a lot behind sofas, in corners … anywhere and didn't really communicate. He was bewildered and traumatised.

Q Do you remember much about that time?

James: I was a walking zombie. I just functioned. My new parents were very good to me but I couldn't feel affection or warmth towards them. I lived from minute to minute with no sense of a future or that what I did affected other people.

Q Did you worry about James, Sue?

Sue: He was much easier than Darren who was very obviously disturbed. James did as he was told, never argued or answered back, didn't damage things. But we became concerned he didn't seem able to make any relationships or friendships. The first Christmas he was with us James ended up sobbing uncontrollably because he couldn't cope with the big family meal. Jim cradled him for about three hours and he really became the mother figure for James. Much later he failed exams he was bright enough to pass and we gathered he would never ask for help if he needed it. He was very fearful of rejection.

Q How did you help James?

Sue: I happened to go on a course about attachment disorder in children and how their whole personality, and their brain structure, is affected by whether they have parents who make them feel safe and secure. If they don't, a classic response is to shut down all emotions and feelings. What I learned in that course ▶

CARE PROCEEDINGS

Sometimes it is better for a child to live apart from their family for a short while, or even for years. There are many reasons why this might be so – the parent or parents may feel unable to cope or the child may have suffered, or be at risk of suffering, significant harm.

REPRESENTATIVES
Where a child is in the process of being taken into care, he/she will be legally represented by his/her own solicitor. In addition, a 'Guardian Ad Litem' (meaning 'your guardian in the court') will usually be appointed to represent the child's needs, wishes and feelings.

THE COURT
The court will probably ask for reports from experts – doctors, social workers and family support workers – to look at the child's needs and whether they can be met by the child's parents or other members of the family – maybe grandparents or aunts. The court will only make a legal order that is in the best interests of the child and must take into account the child's own wishes and feelings, depending on their age.

WHAT HAPPENS NEXT?
If a child is permanently taken into care, he or she may live with a long-term foster family or in a children's home or care home. Some children go to live with an aunt or grandparent. Social workers continue to monitor the child's situation.

explained a lot about how damaged James and Darren were. I went on to do an MA in attachment theory. It was after that time that Jim and James began weekly sessions.

Q So what happened, James?

James: Dad wanted to explore my past with me to help me understand what had happened so that I could move on from just shutting everything off. It's been a painful process because I could never talk about myself and then when I started to do it things opened up and that hurt.

Q So did you go on with it?

James: Yes and in the two years doing this with Dad I have begun to understand what went on. Being neglected by my parents and put with all sorts of foster carers the only way to defend myself against desperation and rejection was to make sure I didn't feel anything.

Q Has that changed?

James: I am able to feel now – I can feel love for Sue and Jim and I understand that they are different to my birth parents and won't let me down. I never used to feel hunger and often I just wouldn't eat, but now I feel hungry. I feel distress and sadness. My parents talk about seeing a change in me. For instance now a sad film gets to me and I am weepy. Before I just laughed at them for being moved. I have started to make plans for my future – for instance to become an IT technician. I'd just have thought that too difficult and backed off the idea, before.

Q So how did you express the pain that came with realisation?

James: I cried a lot exploring why I have been the way I am.

Q So what has followed from this?

Sue: He has taken up Morris dancing which is very special because it means being part of a group and trusting others.

James: We have always watched Morris dancing on Boxing Day in our village. The wife of a dancer invited me to join in and I haven't looked back since. There's no way I'd have done that two years ago.

"We have always watched Morris dancing on Boxing Day in our village. The wife of a dancer invited me to join in and I haven't looked back since."

Q So how does mixing with people and letting yourself get closer feel?

James: I feel I'm respected a lot. I have more true friends than I have ever had and I do believe they would stick by me if I was in difficulties. Once we are close I hug them and let them hug me and stuff.

Q Do you feel you know why you have changed?

I understand that because Dad and Mum have given me security and never stopped letting me know I am wanted, I dare let myself feel again. But there's still so much to do. I have buried my whole past and when for some reason it comes up there is suddenly this pain and I want to block it out again. I just need to leave the past and get on with the present. ■

ADOPTION – THE FACTS

Adoption is when a couple or a single person permanently and legally takes on the responsibility of a child. The birth parents can consent to their child being placed for adoption or a court can decide that it is in the best interests of the child to be placed with a new family. The welfare of the child is always at the heart of any legal proceedings.

LEGAL RIGHTS

Once a child has been adopted, the birth parents no longer have legal rights over that child. Some children are adopted as babies, others as young children. Many older children are adopted by a step-parent. Adoption offers the chance of a stable family life to children who may have spent some time in children's homes or with different foster parents. As much as possible, brothers and sisters are kept together in the same family group.

CARING FOR MY MOTHER

Sauska*, 14, is a carer for his single mother Gillian* who has renal failure. It can be difficult being there for his mother and getting an education.

* Not their real names.

Q When did Sauska become a carer?

Gillian: I had renal failure in 1996 when Sauska was three. I was separated from his father. I started fainting and vomiting. It was a new illness and I was having dialysis three times a week. I relied on a babyminder then, but as soon as he could Sauska took care of me.

Sauska: My first memories are when I was six and Mum and I would be out on the street and Mum would start feeling sick. I didn't understand but I wanted to

"I relied on a babyminder then, but as soon as he could Sauska took care of me."

> "Mum has been put on dialysis treatment three times a week, which usually makes her very tired and she may feel sick and unwell. As she is on her own I have to, and want to, take care of her."

support and comfort her. I wasn't sure what to do. Then there was the occasion a little later when Mum was collapsed on the sofa. I thought she was sleeping so I went to get a video to watch but when I got back she was on the floor and frothing at the mouth. I called an ambulance and went with her to hospital.

Q What has happened since?

Sauska: Mum has been put on dialysis treatment three times a week, which usually makes her very tired and she may feel sick and unwell. As she is on her own I have to, and want to, take care of her.

Q What does that involve?

Sauska: My routine is to make her breakfast with lemon and ginger tea. To get a prescription from the pharmacy if she needs it. If everything seems fine I go to school then, but sometimes when Mum feels so bad she can't get to dialysis I take the morning off school to care for her. I call up the hospital and ask for another dialysis appointment. I phone people from our church – Mum is a born-again Christian – and ask them to pray for her. ▶

Q How much school do you miss?

Sauska: I miss about a quarter of the time but I also miss out on homework assignments and lessons preparing for essays. So I do get behind. It can be hard and there are teachers who think I'm skiving. I don't think there's a great deal of awareness of what's wrong, but then I don't want people feeling sorry for me.

Gillian: He is so good to me. He cooks, cleans, takes clothes to the launderette. I was watching an award ceremony for young carers the other day and thinking Sauska deserves an award.

Q Do you feel very different to other children?

Sauska: I have felt sad watching other children being picked up from school, walking with their parents. At times I have felt I'm carrying a mountain inside me, but I never wanted my mum to see this.

Gillian: I often feel Sauska is protecting me by not saying when he's worried or upset about something, but I try hard to get him to realise it's all right and I can cope. Sometimes we cry together.

YOUNG CARERS

In the UK, around 175,000 young people are caring for their sick, mentally ill or disabled relative. This might involve doing the shopping, cleaning, washing and cooking as well as personal care for the ill parent and caring for younger brothers and sisters. And they still need to go to school.

NORMAL CHILDHOOD?

Although many young carers do not realise how exceptional they are in caring for their parent or parents, others feel all too often how different and isolating their lives can be. The caring duties can leave little time for friendships, schoolwork or relaxation. Some young carers are reluctant to let social workers or people outside the family know what a struggle it can be, for fear that the family might be split up.

SUPPORT FOR YOUNG CARERS

While these young people will never have as free a childhood as most of their schoolmates, there is support available. Several organisations, including The Princess Royal Trust for Carers and the Children's Society National Young Carers Initiative, offer practical support to young carers. They also have good websites that offer homework help or other advice, and also provide links to young carers projects around the country. If a young carer lives close enough to attend one of these projects, it can be somewhere to meet people in a similar position and to have fun. Barnardo's also runs several projects for young carers and their families around the country. If none of these projects are close by, a social worker may have other ideas of how to access support, or additional care, should it become necessary.

Q Do you and your Mum do things together?

Sauska: We go to the cinema or rent a film and have ice cream. We eat out in our favourite Chinese quite a lot.

Gillian: It makes me so sad. I feel the dialysis has prevented me being the adventurous person I am, going to the Caribbean, rafting, climbing rocky mountains with my son. I can only go to countries with dialysis. I tell Sauska he should go with other people, but he says it wouldn't feel good leaving me at home.

Q Have things changed in the years?

Gillian: My health has improved a good deal since I joined the new church with a pastor who is a wonderful healer.

Sauska: She is much happier. Before she was very sad a lot of the time. The church gives me the sense there is someone out there who knows what I am going through and cares about me.

Q What about the future?

Sauska: I can't be sure. If Mum goes on getting better I'd like to go to university and she is absolutely determined I must do that. Also to get married if I want. She tells me fiercely that I must have my life. ■

Q Has being a carer affected your friendships?

Sauska: My close friends know about Mum and understand why I'm not at school. Being a carer hasn't got in the way of making friends.

Gillian: I try to make a normal home life with sleepovers when kids come here. I make jerk chicken and other special dishes and organise it so I have dialysis the day before. I know I'll be okay then. We have a second sitting room so I go in there and leave Sauska and his friends to it.

GLOSSARY

adolescence
The state that someone is in between puberty and adulthood.

adoption
The legal act of permanently placing a child with a parent (or parents) other than the birth parents.

cathartic
Something that makes emotions flood out and relieves emotional tension.

criticise
To find fault with something or someone.

dialysis
A medical procedure to remove wastes and additional fluid from the blood after the kidneys have stopped working properly.

diarrhoea
Frequent, fluid and sometimes painful bowel movements - often a symptom of a problem or disease.

divorce
The legal act of ending a marriage.

Facebook
A social networking website – allowing people to chat to friends, see what they are up to, make new friends and view photographs.

fostering
Where a child is placed temporarily in the care of a person, and during that time the person is responsible for making the decisions for the welfare of the child.

malicious
Having the nature of or resulting from malice – feeling a need to see others suffer.

Morris dancing
English folk dances performed by men and women in costume.

pastor
A minister or priest of a Christian church.

psychiatrist
A medical doctor who specialises in the diagnosis and treatment of mental disorders.

renal failure
A condition in which the kidneys stop working and are not able to remove waste and extra water from the blood or keep body chemicals in balance.

role reversal
A situation where a person swaps the usual role with another - for example when a child starts acting like a parent and vice versa.

separation
When a married couple lives apart. A trial separation occurs when a couple lives apart for a test period to see if they still want to divorce. Spouses are said to be living apart if they no longer live in the same home, even though they may continue their relationship.

visitation rights
The defined periods when a non-custodial parent has times with his or her child.

volatile
A volatile relationship is one that is unstable or explosive and often changes very suddenly.

FURTHER INFORMATION

ORGANISATIONS & HELPLINES

Barnado's
Web: www.barnardos.org.uk
Barnardo's vision is that the lives of all children and young people should be free from poverty, abuse and discrimination. They work with children, young people and families.

British Association for Fostering and Adoption
Web: www.baaf.org.uk
Supports adopting and foster parents and their children and campaigns for better outcomes for children in care.

ChildLine
Young Person's freephone: 0800 1111
Web: www.childline.org.uk
Telephone counselling for any child with any problem.

Children's Society National Young Carers
Web: www.youngcarer.com
Information for anyone who works with young carers and their families.

Gingerbread/One parent families
Helpline: 0800 018 5026
Web: www.gingerbread.org.uk
Offers help to parents on a wide range of matters. They have a range of useful publications.

Missing People
Helpline: 0500 700 700
Web: www.missingpeople.org.uk
A charity that works with young runaways, missing and unidentified people, and their families.

NSPCC
Helpline: 0808 800 500
Web: www.donthideit.com and

www.nspcc.org.uk
A dedicated number if you need child protection – for example if you or anyone you know is being abused.

PACE
Web: www.pacehealth.org.uk
PACE is London's leading charity promoting the mental health and emotional wellbeing of the lesbian, gay, bisexual and transgender community.

Parentline Plus
Free helpline: 0800 800 2222
Web: www.parentlineplus.org.uk
Parentline Plus has 10 call centres and takes thousands of calls from adoptive and fostering families and those in step-families.

The Princess Royal Trust for Carers
Email:youngcarers@carers.org
Web: www.youngcarers.net
Supportive, online community of young carers for discussion or for advice.

Salvation Army
Web: www1.salvationarmy.org.uk
The Family Tracing Service aims to restore (or sustain) family relationships, by tracing relatives with whom contact has been lost, recently or in the past.

Samaritans
Tel: 08457 90 90 90
Web: www.samaritans.org.uk
Support for anyone in crisis.

Single parent action network
Web: www.singleparents.org.uk
An organisation set up to create a voice for single parents and their children and to empower families.

There4me
Web: www.there4me.com
'Email support service for young people between 12-16 years.

Youth Access
Helpline: 020 8896 3675
Web: www.youthaccess.org.uk
Counselling services for young people aged 12–25 years.

Youth2Youth
Web: www.youth2youth.co.uk
Email and telephone support, run by young volunteers for under 19s.

FURTHER WEBSITES

www.bbc.co.uk/parenting
The BBC has a website on parenting covering many key issues.

www.oneplusone.org.uk
An organisation that researches how families function.

www.youngminds.org.uk
The young people's mental health charity.

www.young-voice.org
A charity that researches views of young people. It has a database of 7,000 young people's views on different issues.

www.thesite.org
Articles on young people's issues including health and wellbeing.

AUSTRALIA/NEW ZEALAND

www.kidshelp.com.au
Free helpline: 1800 55 1800

Telephone and online counselling for young people under 25.

www.youthline.co.nz

Support for young people in New Zealand.

INDEX

TALKING POINTS

The interviews in this book may provoke a range of reactions: sympathy, empathy, sadness. As many of the interviewees found, talking can help you to sort out your emotions. If you wish to talk about the interviews here are some questions to get you started:

Alex's story - page 6

How well do you think Alex has adjusted to living two different lifestyles? Is divorce easier to go through for children who have siblings?

Isabel's story - page 8

Isabel didn't understand what was happening at first. How much do you think parents should tell children about their separation? Why do you think Isabel was frightened about not seeing her father again?

Francis's story - page 10

Why do you think Francis's relationship with his father was so bad? Why do you think his mother at first insisted that Francis carried on seeing his father? How could their relationship be mended?

Tegan's story - page 14

Why do you think Christmas can be an unhappy time for separated families?

Melanie's story - page 16

Do you think it's better to have no memory of the family being together, like Tegan, or to be older and witness the separation as Melanie had to? Should teenagers and young adults emotionally support their divorcing parents?

Nell's story - page 18

How well do you think Nell handled the first meeting with her dad? Why do you think she hasn't seen him for six months?

James's story - page 22

Why do you think James couldn't feel any affection for his adoptive family at first? How do you think Morris dancing helped him?

Sauska's story - page 26

Do you think it's right that Sauska has to take care of his mother? What could be done to help him?

These are the lists of contents for each title in *Talking About Myself:*

Depression
What is depression? • All alone • Love's lost • Drug-taking depression • Accepting the past • Years of depression • Managing meltdown - bipolar disorder • Pushy parent • Attempted suicide

Eating Disorders
What are eating disorders? • Recovering anorexic • Fighting bulimia • Reaction to bullying - male anorexia • Dangerous images • Symptom of depression • From obese to bulimic • Fighting obesity • Feeling good at last

Losing a loved one
Coping with loss • Living with guilt • Losing a brother • Keeping a friend in mind • Caring for my mother • Holding on to memories - losing a granddad • Coping with a tragic death • Hearing from abroad • Feeling betrayed

My family
What is a family? • Dealing with divorce • When my parents split up • Father and son difficulties • Keeping the peace • Difficult at any age • Meeting my father for the first time • Care and adoption • Caring for my mother

Racism
What is racism? • Trying to belong - a Muslim's story • Culture clash • Being the outsider • Anti-Semitic attack • Bullied by other Muslims • Breaking down racism • Not allowed to mix • Growing up with racism

Relationships & Sex
First relationhips • Sleeping around • Sex without attachment • Glad to be gay • Dealing with homophobia • Losing my relationships confidence • Becoming a single parent • Young father • Childhood abuse